Flying Tom

1

CHECK-IN COUNTER →

My little brother, Tommy
never stops asking questions.

At the airport,
we took our bags
to the check-in counter.
"Where are our bags going?"
asked Tommy.

"To the plane," said Dad.

"How do they get on the right plane?"
said Tommy.

"They have tags on them," Dad said.

2

Our small bags
went through the x-ray machine.
"What does that machine do?" asked
Tommy.

"It sees inside our bags," I said.

"Why?" said Tommy.

"To see if there are bombs,"
I told him.

"I can't see any bombs," said Tommy.

"No. There are no bombs," I said.

4

We sat by "Gate 16"
waiting to get on our plane.
"When will it go?" said Tommy.
"When will it go? When will it go?"

I said, "Do you have to ask
so many questions?"

Dad said, "It's okay
to ask questions.
If we don't ask questions
we don't learn anything."

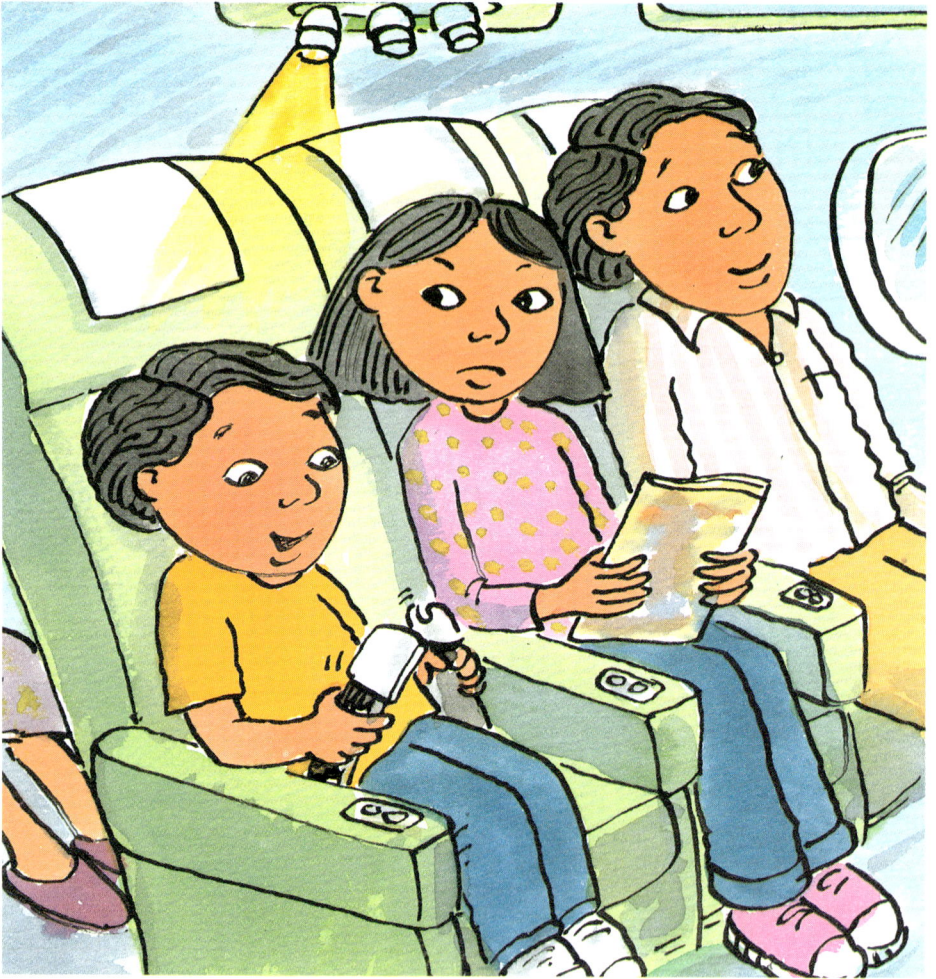

When we got on the plane,
Tommy asked questions about everything.
He asked about the seat belt.
He asked about the light.
He asked about the headphones.

The plane took off.

The cabin attendant came with trays.
"What's that?" asked Tommy.

The attendant put a tray
in front of Tommy.
On the tray,
there was a big sandwich,
an apple, and some milk.
"That is your lunch," she said.

Tommy didn't ask any more questions
for ten minutes!

Mr Cannelloni

Mr Cannelloni
had a little purple plane.

He flew it to Milwaukee
and he flew it back again.

He dived a dive and looped a loop
above a speeding train . . .

. . . then landed in a pumpkin patch
in the pouring rain.

Fire! Fire!

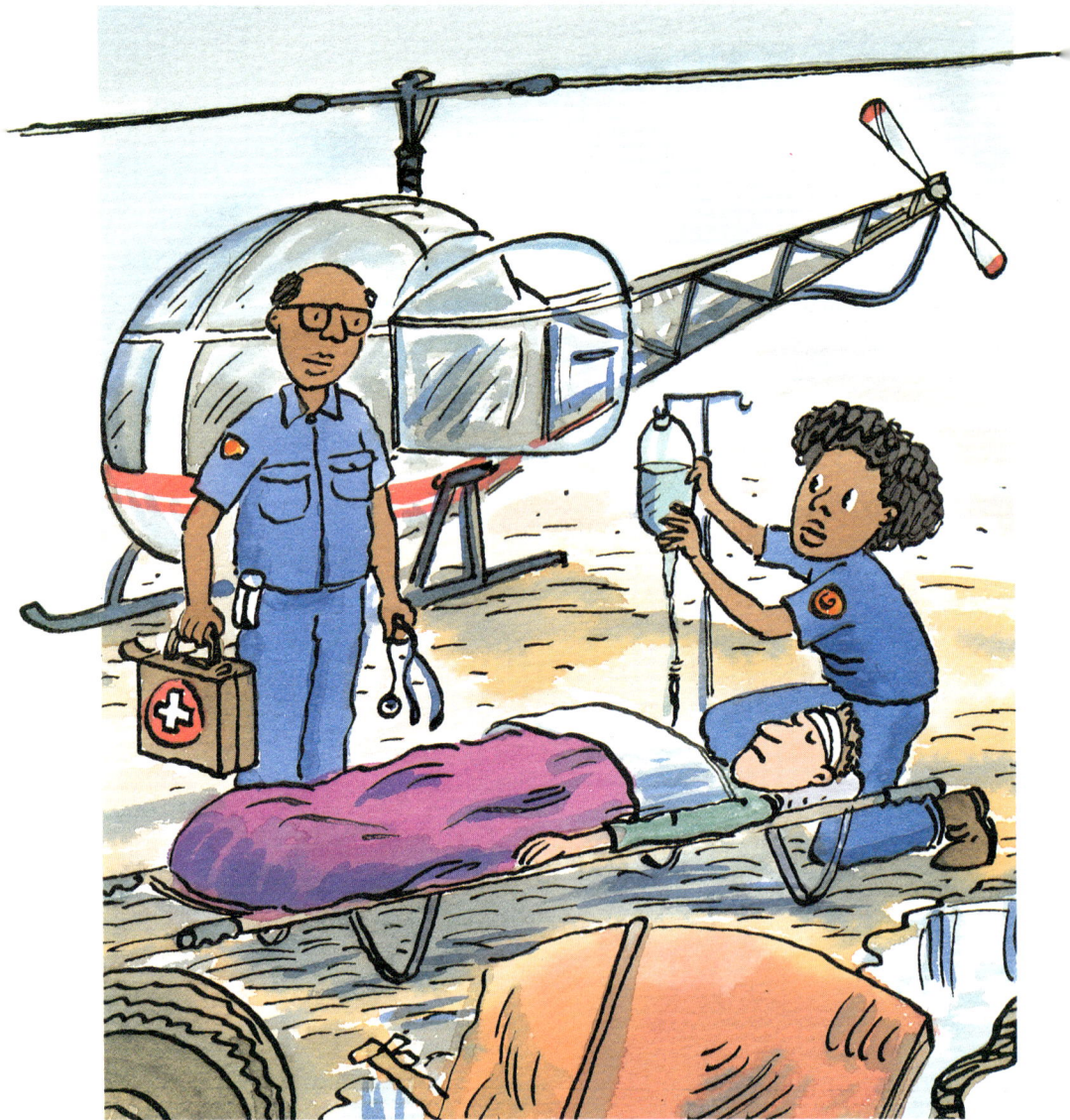

Mr and Mrs Reed are
helicopter pilots.
They fly sick people to hospital.

One day, they got a call
from the fire station.
"A building is on fire!
A man is trapped on the roof!
Please come!"

The Reeds could see
the man on the roof,
but there was smoke and fire
all over the building.
They could not land the helicopter.
It was too dangerous.

Mr Reed put down a ladder
and Mrs Reed flew the helicopter
over the roof.
There was a lot of smoke now
and Mrs Reed couldn't see anything!

Then Mrs Reed saw the man
on the ladder!
She flew the helicopter away to safety
as the building exploded in flames.

"Just in time!" said Mrs Reed.